PLUS ULTRA

Also by Sarah Fletcher

PAMPHLETS

Kissing Angles (Dead Ink Books)
Typhoid August (Poetry Business)
Caviar (Out-Spoken Press)

PLUS ULTRA

SARAH FLETCHER

CHEERIO

First published in Great Britain in 2023
by CHEERIO Publishing
www.cheeriopublishing.com
info@cheeriopublishing.com

10 9 8 7 6 5 4 3 2 1

Typeset in Perpetua by Martha Sprackland
for CHEERIO Publishing

Printed and bound by TJ Books Ltd, Padstow, Cornwall.

A CIP catalogue record for this book is available
from the British Library.

ISBN: 978 1 80081 646 6

Contents

The tragedy of sexual intercourse is the perpetual virginity of the soul.

W. B. Yeats

PLUS ULTRA

Towards Anything of Use at All

Shut up about the pain! You want to make everything
    about the pain!
Fear is far more serious.
Fear is the causal, secret agent –

one morning, every morning. That . . . fear
snuck in like a bayonet onto her tongue.
Of course one deranges themselves into escape.
You would too. *Liar!*

With her leaving (or going? No one
was there to intone
the intention of the moment)
air giggled less mischievously.
There was less information in the world.

With her going (or leaving?
No one was there to watch her final shot,
which was per usual)
air split like gone-off cream.
I breathe two things simultaneously:
one too thin for comfort and one
the clot of the fact of the death
of her curdled brown death.

Then I went for drinks, and forgot the metaphor entirely.
There is less information in the world.

At her flat, we sat on the mouldy sofa. She was old and we
felt pink as the mouth of a viper.
We moved as if time were swallowing us.
Its jaw unhinged and squeezed us towards its pit,
towards the crisis and its cry.

These are the terms of mourning with poison.
You can take them or leave them. No one leaves them.

Shut up about the pleasure! You want to make everything
    about the high!
She sought the level below pleasure.
That which allows one to massage their means
into a greater brilliance,
which for her was making tea. Door knocking at all hours.
Calligraphy. (She couldn't leave the house.)
Her blankets were rotten, and the cop shows on the television
made us feel less paranoid about the cops.

When the seventeen-year-old, too-thin boy told me of her
    death,
I wrote that her life was 'like a sphere of marble being boiled
towards its inherent angel'.

Now I write it is like 'a sphere of marble being boiled
towards anything of use
towards anything of use at all'.

I had to tell George.
He gave me permission to say nothing on the phone
and just breathe,
let my lungs work as if they were submerged in swamp,
in which I then found solace
but now feel only weight.

Then I went for drinks, and forgot the metaphor entirely.

It is braver for us to go on as she had been –
learning nothing
as a protest or a form of love.

Life's expensive, and
most of us are on it
by the time we leave,
or go, regardless.

5

PLUS ULTRA

I

The book is not an image of the world. It forms a rhizome with the world, there is an aparallel evolution of the book and the world.
— Gilles Deleuze & Félix Guattari

Semper fidelis. Lealtad. Rubbish.
Lithiumatic. Obscolene. So weepy.
I'd rather make love to the pearl-endowed harpist.
You will be getting very sleepy.

Her mouth, prostrate and lying, lies,
fingering disaster but never quite.
And then her mouth, which scatters into cries.
What eyes are to a soul, we spend in light.

Orific windows are their own vulgar device.
You must declare. No vermut can change it . . .
You must declare.
                 I am making a sacrifice.
I am a poet. No vermut left. Change it.
So:

PLUS ULTRA the vision of Guernica.
This is the poem I am trying to write.
Blackbird blacked on the blacking surface.
Blacking through the canvas into flight.

C4 TrawsCymru on a Thursday Afternoon

The morning I told you I was to leave for Wales,
I felt
the sense of being removed, like my clothes,
which had been taken to the floor
with suspiciously good care.

I can't explain to anyone, most of all my darling,
the sound Love makes as it crinkles in the morning
like a sheet of wires sliding off our bed
across the crumbs of someone else's wedding cake.

Cordelia

In a stranger's Georgian house   she waltzes with my boyfriend
to Mahler   and tells me about emotional labour   and that I'm so much younger

Her name is so moneyed   I could call her Lulu or Allegra and she'd
respond   When she is tired of waltzing   she twists

her arms around Matthew   who is passing out on the sofa   and says
she can tell I don't trust other women   *no darling   just you*

Her voice is a wire coathanger   I hang what I want on it
but now   the gin stinging my teeth   I just want her to admit

she's taken dance lessons   and who paid for them   She dresses beautifully
like the girl who bullied the school shooter   and in another life

we get cappuccinos and she tells me what sex with my boyfriend is like
focusing mainly on the lingerie she wore   and how she wouldn't let

him touch her until she could tell he was so hot   he would
come immediately when she permitted it   I've never seen a smile so white

as when she tells me how she washed the semen from his stomach
in the porcelain sink   and how many times he said sorry

9

Tender

On the long sip of a train journey
he has hidden twelve pink cherubs
in the body. When he breathes out,
I hear them
                        impotent and wailing
like laboratory mice. Speak English,
children. For my sake, please.
When he breathes in, they scream.
Please be gentler with your breathing,
as I am with mine.

Their heads bulge beneath his skin.
Two have burrowed in his jowl for comfort.
I am not their mother. Not a chance.

When he breathes again, the train roars. I go
Quiet. Quiet! Christsake, Sam. I want to get off.

Beginning Again Without a Title

Or, it was like that field trip in Madrid
(I helped the kids board the autobús
while their tanned dads hid hard-ons
like magician's doves) when you entered my museum
of sneaking looks,
a deck of cards
hidden beneath the garish sleaze
of the sleeviest Spanish guitarist.

Behind glass, the lingering gaze.
Behind more glass, hands holding.

You say of course that you prefer red wine.
Well that's boring. Let's change the scene.

I told him that he has a tacky face.
He didn't even know who Serge Gainsbourg was,
which I tucked into my accumulating hatreds
(a useful tool for later,
like a plastic knife in an asylum).

I am thinking of a mother, my own. She said
I'd make myself dizzy
with my epigenetic love of fizz . . .

that familial tolerance of blurriness,
whether photographs or pharmaceuticals,
that lusciousness of oblivion
so served in cups, or glasses.

People should feel more ashamed.

That slug voice of yours: does it not make you feel
    embarrassed?
You should tuck it somewhere, safely. I have a place in mind.
Or pour salt across the scoundrel.
My kitchen's waiting like a schoolgirl, restless. Cupboards
    scream.

The dolphins and even the seals know.
The spew of froth, like witches' arms,
calls out your name,
which takes on a new terror
when crawling from the water.
You're a bastard.

It isn't you, but the feelings I put on to you:
test-tubed and plain as a noughties model.
The lapse between experiment and Esperanto.

My joy's thinking of you the way a dog
may think of you. Then, I can like you.

This isn't the first time.
The gun is jumped and child crucified.
The gun's implied and child crucified.
Chekhov is dead. The child's long since died.
Sometimes I think: they're just like this.
They are always like this, please let me
be like this, so I can be like them. O look I am.

I find my hands holding my thigh –
like the neck of that rapist swan
set out by feminists –
for eating after hours.

'She conjures neon fairy energy.'
She could kill herself over it. Poor thing.
                        You'd be afraid to even.

By she, of course, O I mean I – but when
seen again the thought comes as a crab
dredged from the darkest pit of sea
– so boil me.

I cough my guilt in little rosaries;
they love my cashmeres and my silks.

They curl like small snails into pearls
to hide from the dynamic of my shame.

Naming the butterfly beneath the impulse
taxidermies the feeling trapped inside.

Like chloroform, casual as sweaters,
is dressed with sins or even inaction . . .

there's still the rosary, each beaded name
adorned without being adored.

How do you send a stranger into sleep?
Here's another glass, a nightcap, maybe.

'No harm, no fowl.'

His long white neck's strung like a line of coke
across a blackened Bible. He is against the sky,

wings of cocaine sprawl
from his slouching shoulders. He's the

fallen soldier falling from his fallen fathers.
A dusting on a book whose author I have killed.

And what of Leda. She combs her hair
on an Aberystwyth beach,
pint in hand. The swan emerges
from the ocean, baring teeth.
She asks him for a fag, and he
extends his beak.

I pursue you like a diagnosis I do not believe in
but still am interested in the medication.

I don't know. Just sweat on me.
Sometimes things exist cerebrally.

Here is a liver. Here's my heart.
I serve them often, these days, with butter.

As long as you can swallow easily,
they go down a treat.

The more you believe in pop lyrics,
the closer you are to God.

Movement in the Fashion of a Magnet

An EKG of a leaf eating a leaf
quietly pulses through my red-blue, leafy dress,
at least four times:

a manuscript quiring the sleeves, or
libidinal velvet brushed quietly back
by the hand-me-not of someone else's hand,

like the Thames' waves retranslating into static, in the
    wind –
all part of the videogame starscape
of my analyst's 'Oriental' carpet,

over which I pull an extremely heavy, dizzying
'Magnet'
across the sewage of patterns, in search of an unpolluted,
    charging line –

to become an alchemist, wringing
algebraic answers from Geometry –
a seeming trick towards Vision,

against all ornamentation.

So why so hard to turn
this 'Magnet'
on the chorus, uninfectious and persuasive?

Many-braided voices
like clasping hands, then beating hands
are a family photograph and

after a family photograph – with their
refrain: from touch, from verse –
damn these prionic, folding repetitions,

acting as membrane, and
registering as shame.

Worthy

Content in rendering the carving,
what paradise will he mine as he lifts

the lid of unhappy cotton? He is jockey
of the slow heart, riding anger down the gangway

saddled with a kiss. I learn it is not
what you want or even what you do but what

you ask for: the vessel of a dark wave breaking
into shivers, a regime of pain cocooning

into your person. Me
and him, the trappings of mercy.

The undesired sun decrees
it's time to go, dragged

across the sky by a fish hook. Kiddo,
these are things we have to learn to live with.

Café Barbieri

When I consider how my *my*
is linked to the orange drink
in a yellow bar. The red curtains. The floor, brown . . .
Do you get the image?

Against mores, quakes and ices
my breath supersedes my tongue forever.
One time, my eminent siren haywired Café Barbieri:
Hands up! But none attend my stick-up, except
John . . . does the police noises as well. It's a set-up.

Anacruses, always, both, to nervous ambience,
though drinking orange
helps, at least ambulatorily.

My *my* auxiliary to my body, his *my* auxiliary to his body.
    Just
like old times.

What good is a bell, full with echoes, false alarms?
My thirst will hush its spaces with these orange swarms.
If you bang me, I will not touch – no, no. Vice versa.
I'm so nervous, I can't remember.

Cheers to John, who understands – cheers John you do –
that to lock my *my* out from the form
of the orange drink
the yellow bar
the salty thoughts of the rough patrons, even the floor,

brown, is
to lock out its scary causes:

the orgiastic dream of God that comes like a flying object,
    spraying
light on everything,
our weak condominiums included!

Madrid Chorus

When he sang, it was with that voice of a thousand hallways,
that I decorated with paintings and silk furnishings and
    parrots,
wine stains on the carpet, and maracas, where we were
    always
just missing the other and this carried on for many years.

Dear Sam, I ask you now – did you get from Love
what you wanted to get from Music?
The sheer fame of it, and something
that grows sweeter and more painful every time?

How you wanted something pure and clear
as melancholy, like high-proof vodka strained twelve times
through silver mesh . . .

And then how you might settle for something less:
alien nausea and literary madness
from a thumb of house red in your glass.

But that also never came.

And the pretty barmaid, the one you loved from Oxford,
eyes off her intellectual, broody duties,
never returned to ask your order.

Did you get from Drinking what you wanted to get
    from Music?

Yes, yes,
more so than love.

Cheers – it is less painful to think of you as dead –
the final chorus bellows down the hall.

Dissociation Boogie

I used to be interested,
interesting.   Ha!

I wore vintage perfume called
                    Traumatique.

And spent four years studying the word
                    Linger.

Scents sang off-key from my skin:
                    Très chic.

I knew what was happening,
what had happened. I was a singer.

But my girlfriends said the zeitgeist
had already grown antique.

Its peak had come, and it smelt boring.
I'm bored as well. Someone is calling.

                    Ha!

Reign

Tatiana wakes ripe, on the flesh
of every bed she's slept in.

Step behind the curtains, Tatiana.
Choose your polis. His voice
is wet: ni droite, ni gauche. Both curio
and spectacle. She peeks through the red silk
that is transversing the room
that is absolutely transversable.

On one side: when I went to Berlin
the Wall
was an uncomplicated ambience.

On the other, living
in a world in which the rain
has lost its instruments.

Epicurean

We tend to gentle foods with gentle hums.
This sweetens the pink salt of hunger's hem.
Montepulciano. Grouse-stuffed hen.
Potatoes like crushed velvet. I *love* him.
We eat at the sore feet of quiet prey.
When he asks me what I think of 'home',
I take little wet bites of things we cannot say.

The Garden of Love's Sleep

After Messiaen's Turangalîla

Dinner is poured. Then   his hand on mine —

instead
of sensation
I receive

the dream
of two green peacocks
pouring smooth grails of touch
each over the other

necks arched in extravagant
romantic love

Insomnia swells a congealing city
congests each head with   phrases:

'A horse called Horus or just Birdy'   'A wine press
    named War on Earth'

Haute contour contraptions from the ancien French
    regime

Áwake   Who is with me?   Whó
will unhook
the colours' ruffles from sunrise
one by one?

When we talk about Manifestos
I feel white

doves sprung from a Magician's
sleeves on sleeves
release

in this state
and at this event

❦

On open caboose   on train to Vladivostok

mosquitoes are breeding quickly in the dark

clouds' petticoats uncross   cross again
flashing the sun from which we cannot hide
which catches us
spoiled and sticky

like Love's Sunday

❦

26

The emperor's clothes are very beautiful   and they are
very real   I remember them like the song
that climbs back to me in snatches:

	Harbouring
the antiseptic beauty	*Harpooning*
the August moon	*Haranguing*
the something something something	*Noon*

Have we slept? I've found us
flabberghastly   clean and glamorose
like the courtesan who appears here
and all other places   in a new state
                  age   dress   civility
having forgot the crashing sound of a beating door
the stench of the night closing in
endarkening   O Carrion!

At last

something beautiful arrives!

The equal weighted phráse
that leaves your mouth and the sky
at the same time

To the Metropolitan Poet

After Tobe

To pull a fleur-de-tulyp from a tankard: presto, magic tric

Those are the pithy quiverings of these nervous spirits
Not quite jostling the unction of my pity

Swimming backwards – no.   If I were, I'd've taken
Them with me, shown them waves ripping
Seams into the British Library

Asked them to deliver the finest flute
From all the stemware   Content
We will not meet againe

Too late   They bathe in the surety
Of the chronicles

Verbiage sewn — — — and left for vex

To treat what so amuses them more uxorio

          how little

Blowjob

I have been to the weighing
Of souls. I have ridden the velvet
Black horizon of American
Highways, shuttling
A Catholic priest
Towards bellies of stars.

I have seen the planets
Purée into streamers
From the drink
And from the
Speed.

An act of service,
An assessment,
Or even therapy.
Violated eyes that become
Clean with your looking.
Host of the divine bistro!
Actor–doctor with the will
To tease the lamb to Easter dinner!
Sing the newborn from a cave!
What did you expect, a rose?

Psychology

When his mouth unfolds   across the quiet of my back
and gives me chills   no amount of love can quell
my fear of what men's minds   wheel out when
a seventeen-year-old girl walks by   In these moments
no kiss can give me comfort   or reassurance
that men aren't looking past me   but rather through
me towards an imaginary sixteen-year-old girl   legs
splayed and smooth as wild eels   so tiny she could disappear

Caviar

Beginning again
at the apple's technology,
like a ninth irradiated life,
I eat the juicy fruit – a top-shelf, porno-picnic moment,
glittering like the piss of a baby rabbit –
to see its inner workings. Bam. Enter. Swiftly: thought.

> (In the back garden, birds start chanting:
> *We're lifting from mechanic sleep!*)

In turn, I chant: *fuck*.
I am handed the plot; I add an I.
Pilot! Pilot! Lift off. Here we go.
The apple's algorithm penetrates.
We fly: zoom, zoom.

Hard-drive, girl-child, rainbow-fish . . .
Consumable tidbits from my dream's wet market.
It all unspirals from my apple-woman mind, the virus,
more impressive than first man, or angel, or circuit.

I feel the fault deliciously,
straining its sensuous motions to the face of God,
fireworking the filthiest collection, moving alively.
I leave the garden, and I reap the world I spawn.

At first the world was fruitful:
            wilful mass theories shooting.
So goes the exponential ticking
            of hateful, playful evolution.

'Life is':
waking
as if moving underwater,
from the only dream
that anybody dreams:
of promiscuity
with dignity, yes, waking slowly,
awash with sweat
on the upstairs couch
of a stranger's party,
rolled in white flannel
and surrounded by empty
baggies and bottles, we are
disgusting little beasts, and moreover
sent into this abattoir
so hungry . . .

> (Interruption: Love Poem.
> I am in Whitstable. Clouds? Used tissues,
> scarred by needles of planes.
> Beach? Empty, awash with footsteps all the same.
> My oyster-mind can connect trifling things in loose
>   systems; no centre.
> You? Beneath the sun's radical surgery,
>   strange-holding
> your face, I see you, smiling.
> We kiss deeply (though the shapes of kisses now
>   escape my mind,
> like imagining a country one's never seen . . .
>   oh my love . . .
> my darling . . . we have no idea what's coming . . .))

I'm ill for weeks. Each dirty image exhausted,
each surface sweat, bones bored with pain,
I take to the spheres. Namely,
that anonymous yellow man
on Google Maps. I drag him to and fro,
to exorcise power over fiefdoms I'll never touch.

I settle on an oil rig, at sea, Caspian Sea . . .
Bulimic waves throw up jetsam's scattered cards.

(Birds are chanting: *dive! dive! dive!*)

So I dive! I am
being haunted by God. Spores of faith.
Stunning plankton
filtering stained glass. I break the black
and the hermetic. Sturgeon-angels,
whose skeletons complete their hi-tech weapons,
triage me into arms. Love.

God reads my mind zoonotically, a thought
so gorgeous I cannot bring myself to choose it.

I climb the velvet lime scaffold even deeper,
colours razed with mounting pleasure . . . I find

God's opera: Real Love. Willing the sturgeons,
those guardians of Eden, living fossils, to sing
lingering chamber music.

How they lap in sorrow's playpen,
their organs knitting together.

And inside those sturgeons
hundreds of eggs: glistened and statutory prayers,
which express exactly what one wants
in the correct language, the first time precisely,
to the correct grant-body . . .
the only dream that anybody dreams.

I mourn the eggs . . .
abducted princesses,
quivers-in-waiting,
packed by the damnéd caravan
into those coils, clean and saved.

> And most beautiful and sad of all
> is how those sturgeons give them up,
> even offer their white stomachs to the surface,
> not from stupidity but trust,
> to poachers with their boorish fishnets,
> who take of this wet, rejected heaven,
> traffic it to oligarchic plates.
> It is entirely my fault . . . but if the men arrive
> I say, amen, amen, and hope
> they are well fed.

Wrapped in paradisal sea, I feel
the opposite of drowning.

Beginning again . . .
I would film myself eating the fruit,
and thus the exponential growth, and thus
the fucking, the contagion, and the
automated journey to the bottom.

Memory, like a jug of evil water

'When I think of my early twenties'
Think first of Camberwell
Never on purpose
And six a.m.
A man

He is
Angry as milk
Slicking himself
A single swan feather
Over full-blown fields of cocaine

Tesco's Finest, 2014

The best of them had made their leave,
which we, of course, had understood.
The tenor between us became too trembling for onlookers.
Things can only sound 'interesting' for so long.
And just our touch was troubling,
more distressing than the bodies left behind,
though Ben promised to perfume them
when he passed our piso in Madrid.
Yes . . . Our touch so troubling that birds fled when we walked
to buy that same Chablis from seven years ago.
Mice cowered when our footsteps shifted in the room.
Who had we left, besides the month-old tobacco
and no lighters and then too many?
Owen took work in Berlin. James left
to make great money out in Cairo.
Georgia stayed but never was the same.
We stopped learning how to breathe:
air wanted to take leave of us too.

The Violet

Translation of a poem by Enrique Gil y Carrasco, 1815–1846

Here I am: a bouquet of past voices.
I sang to flowers, with no bud of my own,
stemming from otherhood of thought. My reckless choices.
Perhaps they wilted underneath my moan.

Here I am: my moan sucked spry and dry.
Shipwrecked for our old love in search of rain.
Shipwrecked from peace and from prosperity.
Watch me in the valley of my pain!

This penance, this pain, is sweet. It's sickly
from hiding so long behind a strong delusion,
which has long since lost its virginity.
My eyes, each day, grow disillusioncd.

Today I return to you, pathetic as a guest
might return to his childhood home,
without the badges, glory, or the crest.
He only comes to excavate the bone.

In dreams that I may sleep with you,
I come to dig up that old skeleton.
Because you heard my voice and sang it true.
Because I saw flesh within your constellation.

It's time to decorate that corpse, you weeping flowers!
While you're at it, embalm me by myself.
Her gorgeous halo ignites its own tower.
Without my love, it lights our plot itself.

Perhaps, perhaps, the virgin of the valleys,
in love and lavish in her own girlhood,
will pass through the shady and written alleys,
where, laid in a grave, she'll find my likelihood.

She will place in her breast with sullen whist,
the cut stem of a humiliated violet.
She cries thus: Poet! Disgraced Lyricist!
This harp of love's already fallen quiet.

The Violet

A version, after a poem by Enrique Gil y Carrasco, 1815–1846

Into the shy plaza
she wore his teflon violet.

There were fake flowers in real soil,
and her gin and tonic drank like a shipwreck.

Listen! A violinist is smearing sound
across the awnings
like a glob of yellow paint.

Whatever we hear in it
is an unburial.

For her:

>*The plastic leaf conceals a hidden world of wet;*
>>*its colour remains locked in weather's debt.*
>*Perhaps taxidermied, or are they dreamt?*
>>*That man before you, have you met?*

And him:

>*Y llorando dirá: '¡Pobre poeta!*
>>*¡Ya está callada el arpa del amor!'*

39

Don't look now!
At least thirteen flies —
their green-black backs!
An oil spill of peacocks! —
are swarming the real fruit of their sangria.

PLUS ULTRA

II

There is always another breath in my breath, another thought in my thought, another possession in what I possess, a thousand things and a thousand beings implicated in my complications: every true thought is an aggression.

— Gilles Deleuze

I met Laura in Camden in the night within the night.
I met her slutty corazón, her opal cur,
and let l'horreur cure us both to eunuchhood
across a powdered mirror.
'You can pay me in Sobranies, or next time bring three
    Valium,' she said.
The aura was Botticellic, ruddy, unguent.
And just that day she called John One or Simon Two
and he delivered her three hundred pounds.
She was there with me,
which meant we were together,
between the high art and the hit.

Overly *there*, with so many organs.
Schizophrenic idol,
between Bridewell
and computer dreams. How many
organs were inside, beating?

Or was it the ice cube, vibrating
softly against the others

in the nearly red rosé, which meant
our drinks were always in a state of movement,
or one of governance?
Or was it the noise
trapped inside the computer
with a fuzz suggesting that it wanted to get out
and then where would it go? Or
the beating like the bleat of the car
of a stranger that I'd entered
and then the beating stuck with me,
inside of us both,
not shared but rather forced –
or the baying of her small, black dog
whose temperament ruled my own
for months. Bark, bark, I said to strangers,
instead of: get me help,
get me the fuck out of this place.
I do not think that I will live
another seven years.

The image and the movement were a veneer
of the sound and the beating bended
the image towards its will.
The beating's will was indefinable and morbid:
shapes and the colours blue and white
and then just blue. Little mobs
reaching their crises.

'Text me when you're safe. I'll put some music on.'

I sipped on the rosé
where the ice cubes continued to suggest

they desired sentience
and wanted to change form
and then where would they go?

Perhaps if she were pretty it'd be easier,
this night within the night.
Then I could dance to the sound
of her liver with a swanful grace.

But night went on and expanded outward for nine months,
crying PLUS ULTRA.
I cried too:
PLUS ULTRA! PLUS ULTRA of having no self-borders!
Which must be like having no mother.
If the latter is the zeitgeist
then the former must be close to home.

After the silver Suzuki, I rehearsed
a sort of mental hygiene that involved
putting names in the place of ideas,
for example, my boyfriend in the place
of phenomenology or Laura
in the place of comfort.

On a mirror, one more time,
I too powdered myself
to eunuchhood,
The Love of My Life subject
to the swelling scene.
Subject objects verb, always:
– semper fidelis.
Here, i.e.: fucking:

————————— sapic concent
————————— orlandish fantasy
————————— morale compass
————————— usurious augury

All things being equal

                       can we do a power couple
in different voices?

                       truth be told I like like you.

Laura is no wigless Corinna courting Covent Garden,
with Swift swiftly buying from her flesh.
She is best when unmanned mans
herself: a true American. I chalk this XX up as static.
XX: the tale end of a disappointing text inside of me,
internalised before I was a me.
O Shame to be an O and not an I.
O shame Oself for O whole life.

O to be a hole

e.g. O pens a canon
O curs
O bays to the whiteish coal

O we
cleaner than a bullet hole.

Returning with my partner, holding hands,
to the crisp cocoons of 'kitten', 'baby',
where there is safety. Spare me.

What else do women watch or:
what do O want? Scratch that: I, I, I am.

   Brekekeekkeke co-ax co-ax Brekekekeek co-ax co-ax

PLUS ULTRA is found carved into a rotted wooden bar top.
PLUS ULTRA beats its stamp so hard
the vermut ripples in the glass of an old lady.
PLUS ULTRA Cortés's son, grifted into Don Juan's army,
vacated from New Spain into Old Spain,
from Castilian to Mexican.
What did he think, misremembering
the ocean's lonesome valley,
as the new planet swam into his kin.
The chthonic ultras of the human sacrifice behind.
The mother, raped. The monarch, waiting.
The father, traitorous
to both.
PLUS ULTRA the whole equation.

The mind that can discover a new flora
can reimagine mathematics:
La Malinche's languages and languishes and anguishes
until it is not language quite. Or language, quiet.

I have seen past the Straits of Gibraltar: PLUS ULTRA.
But so has everybody else.

   Brekekeekkeke co-ax co-ax Brekekekeek co-ax co-ax

Mss Coeur and Mss Bibble . . . shush.
They are speaking. They are speaking

in the hallway.
Their bodies babble together
after the fact. Mss Bibble said
She was a new man after the divorce
'You could say, I knew well their vegetable love'.
'You could say, something melted
and then after, something grew.'
Let's permit a vanitable hush.
Our bodies babble together
like babies in warm water. I am always somewhere,
playing my reoccurring role as someone else's bathtub.

Laura goes to bed with someone else. I think
there must be ice cubes in my blood.

I am aware of everything I've ever loved . . .
that dog from the street – with the ears, not with the
    snout –
scratch that. The dog with the ears.
The God with the snout. Yes, I love all of them.
The gold leaf candelabra at my mother's,
the iron staircase; also my mother.
The first rapist. Even the second. Jesus. Snow-clad trees.
My hair dyed white blonde. My boyfriend. Cigarettes.
I love most that it isn't morning,
when I might dare to rouse to sleep.

They tell me to write it down but this is only a recording:
~~Photography~~ Pornography.
Bark, bark.

Manzanilla and Olives at La Venencia

'Of course, looking into the face, your face,
grief puppets the fact before it's said.
I see . . . O Love! How much more than
a cool drink you count me in . . . Old Love!
How are you this circus mirror
which I see, now, is simply mirror
of my own construction
and reflection, spawned from and breeder of
unalchemical thinking, which is . . . thinking's excess
into which my vision must cascade forward,
and from which sight, I fear, has no return?'

Capitulation

I

Feigning the playfulness
of Mother-may-I   he
asks for a days-of-the-
cane throwback   I
refuse

Back then I tendered my touch
more dearly   I lived in his kiss
for so long I was born in it

Now   an ex-echo   and him
a guerrillista of nettles and wit

I can give him what he came for
and what he now resists

II

The decapitated photograph
of a torso   sexless in
the high contrast   tender in
the anonymous lust-trade
is constant as static to my mind
like my friend describing the
sting her boyfriend draws from
her heels tied and

does she feel like a present
as he tightens the ribbons

so tell me   what is your
luxury and who delivers it

   III

All the milkmaids
inconsequential as achoo have
jostled into wakefulness at his
arrival
they are burning their
hems legs rising like the vim
of popped champagne

he says Thank You
but I did not mean to revive him

you fucking dirty pigeon of a man

49

She was at the Victoria when seeped into her

I was at the Victoria when seeped into me
the brew of something new: the silkworm
spinning silk inside.

The usual thicket of faces
injured the light. And I, as usual, adored
the lager bubbles with their distended stomachs,
the pickled eggs like baby's fists.

Until. The viscous drapery of Guinness
loomed towards me in the glass:

a scallop's single foot
towards midnight's trench
in search of something that gives birth to itself.

Washing at the End of the Night, Which Is the Next Day's Afternoon

A foot, my own, can be either
collaborator or accessory to a cause,
especially when looming its sole
across the surface of a bath to gauge the heat.

A woman's foot, when shed from fishnet tights, is
    a free fish,
a small gesticulator, circling toes to ripple.
This is foreplay for the end of Progress . . .
Hush now; it is entering the whirlpool,

which sucks us to a refracted world.
Enter a garden, where the air writes it all down.
Nymphs, washing; sororal twins
to stiff Greek columns. Gowns as melting candles.

Exhausting to find the universal in this caper.
Psychic hygiene in a restored Venetian arch.
Temperature is perfect. Water, perfect.
I am empty. I have killed my mother in myself.

Office Poems

The second betrayal, of course, comes as

the disintegration of a 'proven history':

each officiated day
is leapt from rapidly: one quick
immersive island
to the next.

Lunch is

the arrhythmic hour is
island number five an
abattoir with floors of sand
lunch the lucid dream job
upsetting order's fluency
I send another email menially
consider coffee
eye my deskscape's
little illnesses
I send with every byte
the weight & filth
of my humiliated heart

Desk Lunch

When I lock eyes with a man
I fold myself into a bill;

I consume the violent foods to balm my mind
and make me more precise;

veal; offal; any taken baby;
the zest of being twin-livered momentarily.

The trick is to identify with it
to make it more delicious;

my tongue lines with a silver sense of dreaming;
one day I will look back to assign intentions;

colourising photographs of wars.

❧

Unfurling ahead of me, no highway of sand or sea

rather
Uriel's wing
the span of my assigned future
guiding me towards
island (six).

First
I dwell in the exilic ecstasy!

Before the angel steers himself
towards seapoint's mouth.

O co-regent of the sun!
Take me with you! Let me in!

❧

An email and its reply is a flower tattooed on a flower

I am against senses entirely: swim, my
puppy-piled heart, or simply
I have been here too long (island seven).

I lap in the gap between my maker
and the one who gives me orders.

Amen: he is so woof
he is productive member
label inmate

❧

Instead of an exit, or a hallway, the door opens to find

every swan at St James's Park
dead from overbreathing in the office Yes my office
tessellated by the orange tooth on brittle sand.

Excitement bejewels too-moving sky,
rich with guillotines of fleshy air

Lads

With them, sex feels like miming drowning.
Gaped mouths gasping, their rower's arms
too heavy from the drink to pull them back
to shore, the thrashing, the feeling
of being below the surface, the grabbing.

& waking next to them in morning,
the bed having spat back their sleeping bodies
to the sun, having fished them into sobriety
like a plastic bag wrenched from a river;
when they are on their backs and gorgeous
like funeral home corpses –
this is when they are most beautiful;

before they wake into themselves,
become one in a thousand boys
named Ollie, repeating tales
about the time they spent at Radley,
lifting their glasses to the rugby
on the telly, left to rehearse
their deaths-by-water nightly
with a girl they will call easy.

The Oldest and Saddest in the World

And O my keen amigo at our breaking
– borders crowded, dam overspilt,
cleaving darkly on heaven's waters,
which are most certainly made of tears and
awash with sturgeons, perhaps
the oldest and saddest sturgeons in that world . . .
– we begin to listen to those suspect channels,
which diagnose our synchronic state, and,
thin singer, this moment, what source?

A pendulum of golden faith:
the chastity
of many leopards:
grandiose, superstitious
and so casually touched
by Jesus' black fingertips . . .
Glowing and reminiscent
of chronic disease,
they slick themselves against the golden hieroglyphs.
And O my pallid sailor, we know that to watch them

in their deep and secret play
is to be an onlooker upon our own most hidden shames.
How beautiful it is, welling in this parasocial love,
to witness real affection among beasts,
unobscured by hunger.

Words Relayed in a Café in Acton, 2017

'When I had my termination,
– the nurse's word – I forced
myself instead to say *abortion*

to remind myself so much of the world
would throw stones across my back
or burn my tongue, or pray
my death would lead me to such places

and in knowing that, felt
the happiness I failed to find in love
swim through my body –
two thousand minnows underneath
a frozen lake. How hate is unconditional,
constant, and easy

like – in any country, at any time,
in Hammersmith or Medellín –
the murder of a woman by her husband,

or, in rarer cases, by her brother,
or her father, or her lover.'

Geometry Playground over Wyoming

After a photograph from NASA of stars named after girls

There are ten little girls on the left.
There are twelve, meanwhile, on the right.
The cowboy moon giddys-up towards morning.
These are Unbalanced Constellations. Petticoats aside.
The symmetry was born this way. Born wrong, not right.
The little girls are fixed as night is dark and cold and dry.

They cannot seesaw into balance, though they try.
It'd be so fun if they could. They can't.
The scientists already named them, though they say
the images are doctored 'beyond belief'.
When morning comes, they all go *Wheeeeeeeee.*
But quietly, or else they'll wake the horsies.
And darkly, lest they give light to prisons.

If only they could hold each other's hands, instead
of twinkling like the twelve tubes of a chime.
They do not have the foresight to be sad:
they think the way a star's supposed to feel.
And O! the things these girls will never see! Such as
the most beautiful sunset you have ever seen.

A Slap in the Face . . . of Nature

Heat
bends through the 'party room'
like a tropical snake. Our drinking amps
the creature's red, systolic turnings.
We are arriving to night's final station.
C'mon babies. Time to ride.

A man in a black bear suit sees a woman in a brown
     bear suit.
Second thought. He doesn't see her. He has followed her.
Through summer's fluffy mists he smelt
her daybed, sussed the perimeter of her desire.
He'd known of her urine for years. A perfect match.
He zips his fluffy suit, and enters through her window.

Swans drinking white wine
are just called swine.
He is
explaining the subtraction
between event and labour value.
Operette. Acropolis. Fawns fawning.

So bored, I tend the moon's aquarium.
Tears turn to teeth of serpents
when they reach the water. Now there are lots of snakes.

They arch their delicious heads for breath.
They want to slither back to my eye's worm-womb,
O linger Sapphos of the lash-line! Please don't leave!

He grabs a girl one by the neck and bites its head.

I'll give you details if you want. He was so slang.
He was circus.
He
bodied me his body.

Why do forty-year-old narcissistic cokeheads
always want to slap me in the face?

It feels overly specific and obscene
to include a pronoun. It pours a drink. It pours
me
a drink.
I drink it.

I'd rather be
summoning angels.
Not angels but haloes.
Not haloes but the idea of haloes.
The idea of a woman,
dreaming of haloes.

When he slapped me in the face
he was Francis of Assisi
preaching to a bird.
Francis of Assisi
blessing a bunny.
He put his fat thumb in a hole in my tights
and pulled. Ladders like lightning up my thigh:
Francis of Assisi
calling thunder.

He is slurring something something partner while
someone is in Camden saying something
something boyfriend. How does she dress?

I take comfort in the deaths of species.
Plants. Gone. Yes. All the plants.
Nervous systems no longer so nervous.
He changes the music to my favourite song.
C'mon baby, time to ride.

I am digitally reincarnated into the past;
born backe as Baudelaire's petty whores.
All of them. Yes. All the whores.

To You with a Guitar

Guitar uncrinkling any sound: the
cough, the rough of papers in that
lady's bag
as she shifts to cross her legs.

Of course,
I worry
about the hazards

of breathing in so much
noise. What can you do
but hope that it will
scrape you clean?

Let it in,
a rod threaded with
cloth, jabbing up a
flute's nose.

To another poet, even you,
living inside this sterile throb
could be like living under God;
God
I agree; I
want it to last forever –

the future mistakes and yawns:
a word.

A woman hit. A nuclear bomb.
The messenger will suffer well, make no
mistake: I am checking in.

You have ghostwritten this poem from ten years in
     the future
and you have ruined my life.

Recounting Gabriel D'Annunzio's Conquering of Fiume in a London Pub, 2019

Vauxhall's adverts turn their dials westward.
Mean time passes quickly.

The Royal Oak, Élan is perfuming Fiume's
final ashes –
he wears the uniform, duenduous black,
and sings with his guitar

Gramsci, do you remember?
Lenin, do you remember
when you toasted Gabriel
with pots of caviar?

Cocaine's sumptuous petticoats remember:
did you think this play?
Who forgot their lines?
Ashes, ashes rebirth into embers.

O citidelphic London,
with tomatoes, lions, lilies:
orgy of the carnival
forging opera . . .

Here is a radical aesthetic for the new bohemians:
your future in a stork's foreigning basket
dropped in the desolate lap
of the Mediterranean.

For Rilke in the Cotswolds

Why here I am I do not know.
The fog's technology obscures not only sight
but meaning. I see wet, tangled fingers, shedding leaves.
Fog passes through them: are they learning?

This time it's come damper, and with
the sound of a seashell crouched against
an infant's ear. What blood-echo am I inside?
Its circulation hides the mother-moon.

Fog has no gender but many children.
It decides what to reveal. How blasphemous.
I'm unprepared to breathe the implications
of a morally neutral discourse. My lungs have motives.

It filters my coat, and my body, which is
also my thoughts. There is no border
to my vision: just fuzzy seams it
threatens to unpick.

I have already said that I am sorry.
I have truanted the holy spirit.
Let myself be haunted by myself alone.
Fog calls me now, as dense as Hebrew

and overwhelming as prophecy.
I promise I – my life – will change.

Violation and Volition

Onlookers compose
the illustrated autotome:

> *she is carried away*
> > *in an ecstatic trance*
>
> *and seized*
> > *to cleanliness.*
>
> *Wading, flashing*
> > *daffodils entrance*
>
> *the air.*
> > *Yes, yes*
> > > *she is there.*

The Bed Is Not a Window, the Bed Is a Two-Way Mirror

Have we met?
Has sleep, its arguments, ornaments, glyphs,
brought you too here . . . to wink with me
before we put back our bodies?

Sleep . . . is jungled by these licks
of tentacles. Sleep
is dragged by bad dreams' jellyfish. Perhaps
we met. Perhaps you glimpsed a personality.

The poet to the reader: you don't know me!
The reader to the poet, painstakingly, repeats:
you do not know me! Is it affirmation, argument, echo?
This is no relationship! This is escape-artistry!

PLUS ULTRA

III

CONSCIOUSNESS has no climax
         — Mina Loy

On the second night within the night,
El Despertar put on a magic show
and while the woman in red feathers danced
there was suddenly, everywhere,
PLUS ULTRA so I turned to the barman and I asked:

Can we unforge the failed necromancy of lineage?
This is the point to which I will always return,
more than the vermut or Guernica.
This is the point.

The O! The pulling names out of a hat
with the feigned surprise of a womannequin
cut in half with a musical saw.

An electric blue dictionary painted nauseously over
with pink. Why not insist on a backward prism
turned upward with maniacal laughter?

and to the dancer I picked up a feather
and stuck it in my drink and I sang
using her mouth, which tasted sweet:

My heresy of -esses!

riding souped-up cauldrons
while going hungry to the Eagles.
They will eat your liver
and can't even make pâté.
They can't even do anything with fire.
Be-which, for your etymology is arriving from the future.
It is carrion. You are ripe.
Woo-hoo, witchy woman,
See how high she flies.

The men will burn pine perish with their own unsustainable vision.
The insulated mind that cannot circumnavigate the circumstance.

PLUS ULTRA fills our drinks, and I am happy, so I drink it all.

We find ourselves here, with duel allegiance
to the incenstual conversation or blank blank happiness of
    the chorus.
Echoed voices in the night,
She's a restless spirit on an endless flight.

Still. We are better nunned than numerous.
Industrious things! Resourceful flowers!
My cabal of productive tenderness:
– you animate the world with sickly weirdness
~~Re~~productive. Recreational. Fuck Daddy.

And to the barman, I lament:

Agon, again, who sings in me? A guy.
A friend whose work has come to nothing.

A black bird blacking into flight.
The difference engine chugs along.
This is the poem I am trying to write.

I was drinking vermut with my favourite girlfriend when
PLUS ULTRA sickly dimorphism.
The cats. The dogs. The moon.
No, not the sun. That stays.

PLUS ULTRA the masculine birth of time
and that action man Adonis with his
autotune, his grifts, mincing his vibes.
The sluiced cannon and its ammunition.

PLUS ULTRA beyond measure
PLUS ULTRA the city limits.
Hypnomania and the
prognosis of allyship.
PLUS ULTRA fucking the mirror
and being in my nap while we dream.
PLUS ULTRA lemon-flavoured fingernails
PLUS ULTRA these dwindling things.

Old this life Old this kiss Old this sweetheart Young the fish
We are crossing the city limits.
We are arriving at the diet of light.

We must return
We must return
We must return to so much
faster.

Notes

p.vii   The epigraph to the book is taken from a quotation by W. B. Yeats, and refers to him finally consummating a twenty-year-long obsession with activist and occultist Maud Gonne in Paris.

p.6   *Guernica*, the 1937 mural by Pablo Picasso, is currently housed in the Museo Nacional Centro de Arte Reina Sofía in Madrid.

p.11   The Leda in 'Beginning Again Without a Title' is, indeed, the Aetolian princess and mother of Helen.

p.18   The beginning of 'Café Barbieri's first line is borrowed from John Milton's poem on his blindness.

p.25   'The Garden of Love's Sleep' takes its title from a movement in Messiaen's Turangalîla.

p.28   'To the Metropolitan Poet' takes its title from a poem by Toby Martinez de las Rivas.

pp.37-8 'The Violet' is a translation (and a version) of a poem by Romantic Spanish writer Enrique Gil y Carrasco (1815–1846). I found this poem in its original Spanish in a small anthology bought second-hand in Barcelona.

p.41   The epigraph to 'PLUS ULTRA II' is taken from Gilles Deleuze's *The Logic of Sense*.

p.44   Corinna is a reference to the rather cruel satirical poem 'A Beautiful Young Nymph Going to Bed' by Jonathan Swift. • Laura being referred as 'A true American' might echo 'To His Mistress Going to Bed' by John Donne.

p.45   The swimming planets are inspired by Keats' 'On Looking into Chapman's Homer'. • La Malinche was a Nahuan woman who was the interpreter, slave, advisor, and eventual consort to Hernán Cortés during his conquest of the Aztec Empire. • The Straits of Gibraltar are flanked by two large rocks that are referred to as the Pillars of Hercules. It was believed that they marked the furthermost limit reached by the Ancient Greek hero. In the Renaissance era, they became synonymous with the warning 'Ne plus ultra': *nothing further beyond.* • 'Breke-keekkeke co-ax co-ax Brekekekeek co-ax co-ax' is the cry of the frogs in Aristophanes' *The Frogs.* Their chorus is a constant agitation to Dionysus. • Mss Coeur and Mss Bibble share a similar dynamic to that of Lil and her friend in T. S. Eliot's *The Waste Land.*

p.46   On an early draft of *The Waste Land*, Ezra Pound writes 'Photography?' in the margins of a section containing reported speech of a hysterical woman.

p.52   'Office Poems' were written with Frank O'Hara's spiritous 'Lunch Poems' in mind.

p.62   'To You with a Guitar' was written after a performance by guitarist Sean Shibe. Specifically, his performance of 'Lad' by Julia Wolfe, which was originally written for nine bagpipes.

p.64   Gabriel D'Annunzio was a decadent Italian poet, nationalist and soldier, whose views went on to inspire Benito Mussolini. He founded the state of Fiume in 1919, now in northern Croatia. The state, which held music as a central governing principle in its constitution, became a haven for revolutionaries, bohemians, homosexuals, and party-goers across Europe.

p.65   The final line of 'For Rilke in the Cotswolds' is a refashioning of 'Archaic Torso of Apollo' by Rainer Maria Rilke. There is also a nod to Geoffrey Hill, who wrote in 'Speech! Speech!' that 'Poetry aspires / to the condition of Hebrew'.

p.68   The epigraph to 'PLUS ULTRA III' is taken from Mina Loy's 'Aphorisms on Futurism', which was first published in 1914.

p.69   The witchy woman in the song lyrics is from the 1971 Eagles song.

Acknowledgements

I'd like to thank the arts organisations and prizes that helped me when I was starting as a writer: the Writing Squad, Foyle Young Poets Award and Tower Poetry.

Thanks are due to the following publications in which poems in this collection have appeared: *New Statesman*, *Poetry London*, *The London Magazine*, *Rising*, *The White Review*, *The Poetry Review*, *Wild Court*, *Stillpoint Magazine*, *The Scores*, *bath magg* and *Hotel*.

Thanks must also be given to the publishers of my three pamphlets: *Kissing Angles* (Dead Ink, 2017), *Typhoid August* (Poetry Business, 2019), and *Caviar* (Outspoken Press, 2022).

This book would have been impossible without the faith and shrewd editorial eye of Martha Sprackland, and the wonderful team at CHEERIO Publishing.

There are many people who, along the way, have given me pastoral support, literary advice, and, at times, true love. I would like to acknowledge them now: Adam, Alex, Alice, Bret, Carlos, Ed, Emma, Eoin, George, Georgia, Maxwell, Mimi, Phaedra, Sam, Sorcha, Steve, and more.

A book of this nature is not something I feel is a compliment to dedicate to someone. Still, I want to highlight the importance of my mother in my writing life and life in general. Thank you for tarot readings, wonderful clothes, coffees in the morning, bucket-filling conversations, and belief that you had given birth to a poet from the moment I was born – and even a bit before. Thank you so, so much for your support over the years. This never would have been possible without you.

Any resemblance to real persons, living or dead, is both premeditated and coincidental.